LEADING REMOTE TEAMS

Embrace The Future of
REMOTE WORK CULTURE

ALEXIS GERST

Edited By: Nicole d'Entremont
Cover Designed By: Kerry Watson

FIRST EDITION

This book is dedicated to:

Briana, my mom and best friend for life: the woman who taught me to lead boldly.

And, to Ryan VanArtsdalen and Jondavid DuVall of the Logistics Officer Association, who recognized my passion project, Leading Remotely, as a valid message worth sharing. Without them, this book may not exist.

Table of Contents

Introduction

When the coronavirus pandemic sent everyone home to telework in March 2020, I was a Supply Chain Logistics Manager leading a team of nine cross-functional team members. Although some of my team members took advantage of teleworking one or two days per week, the leap to full-time telework was a shock to us all. My military leadership training kicked-in and I embraced my digital comfort as a millennial to take full advantage of remote work tools. I rapidly transitioned all of my team's regular activities to a virtual format, and we quickly pivoted to the telework environment. We led the way and established the 'new normal' within our organization to operate digitally and continue our mission.

Just four months into the pandemic, I transferred to a new organization as a Program Manager. This transition happened nearly all virtual. The only time I went into the office was to meet my new supervisor and collect my assigned computer. As I navigated the transition to work with a large team of people I had never met before, I took note of my feelings in the transition along with observations about which practices seemed to work and which ones didn't.

What I didn't realize at the time of this transition was how many other teams struggled to transition their collaboration activities, keep the lines of communication open, and reinvent themselves remotely. Talking with others, I learned just how much most people struggle to transition to new teams and/or bring new hires onto their team while teleworking—especially the 'more seasoned' generations who are less comfortable in the digital environment. The commonly heard refrain was, "Things will get better once we get back into the office".

Now over a year into the pandemic and working remotely, *it is clear that things will never really go back to the way they were.* Many employees will work remotely at least part of the time and getting the entire team together in the office may be rare in the future. Now we know how well we can work remotely. Pandora's box has been opened.

This book will take you on a journey beyond average office leadership and into the high-performing realm of remote leadership. We will discuss why leading remotely matters in the context of current events and why we are unlikely to go back to the way things were. I'll cover the advantages to both employees and the employer. Then, we will talk about trust as a critical piece to remote leadership and how to build a strong foundation of trust and connection on your remote team. I will deliver tactics you can execute to bring your team together and make progress on the outputs that matter most to your organization. Lastly, we will cover tips for clear and effective communication in the digital environment before wrapping it all together with my vision for the future of remote work.

As a "thank you" for reading, I'd like to invite you to download the audiobook for free. You can access your free download of *Leading Remote Teams* by going to www.alexisgerst.com/audiobook.

My goal for this book is two-fold. First, I hope

this book gives tactical and mid-level leaders tools to improve their digital leadership skills and lead their teams to thrive in a remote work environment. Second, my wish is for organizational leaders at all levels to adopt the opportunity and advantages remote work offers.

Together, we can embrace the future of remote work culture.

Part I: Why Remote Leadership Matters

Chapter 1: Remote Work is Here to Stay

We thought it was just temporary. Only a quick work-from-home stint. Two or three weeks, maybe a couple months—maximum. Then we would be back in the office. When we went home to telework, no one imagined that one year later…we would still be working remotely. The coronavirus pandemic changed the work environment paradigm in America and around the world as companies flexed and adapted to the new demands of society.

After overcoming the discomfort of learning to do something different, we now realize we can still function—in some cases even more efficiently—with remote work as a substantial piece of the new corporate structure. Demand for remote leadership skills and experience will surge. Even if you plan to work primarily from an office building, you will likely soon lead team members across town and even throughout different time zones.

What is Leading Remotely?

The idea of remote leadership can be confusing at first. If you are not yet familiar with remote work, telework, or work-from-home options, then remote work might conjure up a picture of someone working in their pajamas on the couch or sitting on the beach with their laptop. Even if you are not guilty of either offense, you can still be a remote leader. Leading remotely doesn't require managing a team across continents, but there are a few key traits.

If your team operates virtually the majority of the time, you are a remote leader. Leading remotely applies when any of the members of a team, including the leader, are not located in the same physical location while working. Perhaps your team is based in a different city than you. If you previously worked in an office most of the time and now telework the majority (or all) of your hours, you are leading remotely. You employ remote leadership even if you still work in an office, but members of your team telework several days per week.

But, you don't have to be a supervisor or even a team lead to lead remotely. When you influence the behavior of others geographically separated from you (whether across town or on the other side of the world), this is remote leadership too. The reality is, many of us may go into the office on a regular basis, but we still lead remotely in today's connected world. You may have clients, customers, contractors, peer organizations, or other contacts in physical locations around the world you communicate with on a regular basis. If you are communicating across digital media to people or contacts you've never met or rarely see in person, you are leading remotely through your digital communications with those people.

If you work with others via telework across a digital platform, the ideas in this book will be useful to you.

Remote Work Might Not Be a Choice

We may not be able to choose between teleworking or going into the office. In fact, situations beyond our control might force us into telework even when we're not ready. Think back to the end of March 2020. Hordes of knowledge-based industry (industries which are based on intensive use of technology and/or human capital) workers who previously were content typing away at their keyboards in cubicle farms were sent home to telework because it was no longer safe to keep large numbers of people in the same area, touching the same surfaces, and breathing the same air. Social distancing became necessary to slow the spread of the coronavirus pandemic, and remote work became status quo.

Office workers around the world struggled with this transition, as they weren't previously accustomed to using digital tools for their regular work activities. Some old-school managers didn't know how or where to set up a conference call because they all just gathered in the conference room or someone's office for meetings previously. Others were familiar with conference calls but challenged by video conferencing, spotty coverage, webcam difficulties, and lack of high-speed internet for some team members. Employees were confused, frustrated, and unsure of what to do. They were told to 'standby' or 'hold on' while organizational leaders 'figured things out.' They said, "This should only be a temporary arrangement for a few weeks while this pandemic settles down."

Weeks turned into months, and months turned into nearly a year before vaccines started rolling out. Some employees transitioned into new jobs during this time, and supervisors hired new employees. Workers new to the idea of teleworking needed someone to tell them what to do and how to do it, yet few stepped up to fill the void. Employees who couldn't adapt quickly to change and even now face issues on how to connect in a digital space. Still, far too few leaders embrace the challenge and opportunity remote work offers.

Even hiring organizations squirmed about the onboarding process and how to bring their new team members up to speed on what they do, plus instill the company culture in new members without seeing their face. Working in a digital environment where social cues, charisma, and body language represent the majority of nonverbal communication, we miss out on the richness of communication and professional human connection.

The commonly heard refrain during this time among teams and employees was, "Things will get better once we go back into the office." Now a year into the pandemic and working remotely at the time of writing this book, *it is clear that things will never really go back to the way they were before.*

People are now becoming accustomed to the flexibility and convenience that comes from teleworking, and it is unlikely employees will want to go rushing back into the office if they have a choice. Further, while we might be able to manage the pandemic and lower the risk of infection through various factors such as wearing masks, social distancing, and vaccinations, it could still be a very long time before the risk is truly low enough to gather large groups of employees in the same location on a regular basis.

Individual contributors, managers, and directors for knowledge-based industries will continue to work remotely, at least some percentage of the time. As more organizations expand remote work practices, getting the entire team physically together will be a rare occurrence in the near future. A survey in the midst of the pandemic found that "almost 70% of full-time workers in the United States are working from home during COVID-19."[1] It is likely that we will still hold almost all of our meetings virtually going forward because team members will be dispersed in different locations. The pandemic expanded options for working remotely, and there may still be restrictions on gathering capacity in the future. Even if you can get half of the team in the office, the other half may be teleworking.

Working in a digital environment is the way of the future. For success in a digital environment, we need to adapt our leadership methods to thrive and reinvent our teams in this setting.

---

[1] (OWL Labs 2020)

The Evolution Toward Remote Work Culture Has Accelerated

Before the 2020 coronavirus pandemic forced organizations and companies to accept remote telework, several jobs within the private industry were already shifting to this model and offering remote work options. Even some government agencies that didn't offer remote-work options before began including working from home one or two days per week. Executive leaders were reluctant to trust their employees to telework, but a leap of faith was forced by social distancing orders. The pandemic left them no choice, and most were pleasantly surprised to see their organizations performing just as well—if not better—than before.

Remote work has been around since the 1970s, and the culture continued to gain traction before the global pandemic, but the pandemic accelerated its momentum. Companies now have a much more positive view of telework: "A Gartner, Inc. survey on June 5th of 127 company leaders, representing H.R., Legal and Compliance, Finance, and Real Estate, revealed 82% of respondents intend to permit remote working some of the time as employees return to the workplace…Nearly half (47%) said they intend to allow employees to work remotely full time going forward."[2] Even the government—notorious for sloth-paced change—is catching on to the telework trend: "About one-third of Air Force employees may remain largely out of the office

---

[2] (Baker 2020)

even after the coronavirus pandemic subsides, Vice Chief of Staff Gen. Stephen W. Wilson said Sept. 16."[3]

The myth that remote employees can't be trusted was busted. The truth is now out. It can't be put back. We can't un-know that success IS possible when working remotely. Very few tasks ACTUALLY need to be accomplished in the office. And for those few tasks that do, a company could easily pay a few days travel per year for the employee to take care of what needs to be done onsite.

Now Pandora's Box has been opened, so we can embrace the advantages of remote work and usher in a new era of flexible work options.

---

[3] (Cohen 2020)

Chapter 2: Advantages to Remote Work

By now, I probably don't need to sell you on the benefits of working remotely. We have already experienced these gains with the great majority of full-time workers in the United States teleworking in some capacity in the year 2020. Despite the communication challenges and some frustration that comes with operating in a different physical location from your coworkers, the benefits far outweigh the challenges.

Remote work can make us more flexible, resilient, and effective when it comes to accelerating change and adapting. This is just as true for the government and military as it is for the private industry. While some jobs may require in-person work, many of the knowledge-based positions have the ability to operate completely within the digital environment. Everyone must keep their mission moving forward, whether that means delivering products, developing software, providing customer service, conducting training, or managing contracts or people. When a company or organization fails to deliver results, they will become obsolete, and their services will no longer be required.

The purpose of this book is to help you overcome the challenges of working and leading remotely so you can take full advantage of these benefits.

In case you thought I'm just championing telework so I can work in my pajamas, let's look at these benefits for both the employer and the employee.

Employer Advantages to Remote Work

Companies who employ telework flexibility enjoy many advantages. Some of them include talent acquisition and retention, extensive cost savings by reducing expenses, improved employee productivity, safety, and continuity of operations.

Talent acquisition and retention is one aspect getting employers excited about integrating remote work options because voluntary employee turnover is costly. According to Gallup, "The cost of replacing an individual employee can range from one-half to two times the employee's annual salary – and that's a conservative estimate."[4] Before, a prospective hire for competitive talent acquisition would need to be willing to pick up and move their entire family and life to a new location, often in another state. On the employer's side, they might have to foot the bill for moving expenses to get the absolute best and brightest candidate working for their company.

Now, human resource departments can recruit across the country or the world without having to add the "must be willing to relocate" clause to their job advertisements. This widens the talent pool of applicants who would be willing to consider a change of jobs to work for a particular company. When you remove the

---

[4] (Mcfeely and Wigert 2019)

filter of location, it increases the level of competition, both for employers and employees. It also increases the likelihood the employer can find the ideal candidate for their position, and it increases the likelihood the employee can find a job that matches his or her skill set and passions. Recruiting from around the country and allowing location-independent work allows organizations to hire candidates who might not otherwise be considered, thus promoting diversity and inclusion.

One demographic with a lot to gain from location independence is military spouses. With the military constantly moving their family, military spouses are one of the biggest groups of unemployed and *under*employed talent. In a time when being a dual-income household is more of a need than a want for many families, one of the most pressing challenges for military families is "staggering unemployment (24%) and underemployment (31-51%) among military spouses, rates that have held for years despite hundreds of millions of dollars spend by the US Department of Defense (DoD) to address the issue and a complex network of nonprofit support."[5] By offering location-independent work, organizations can contribute greatly to improving this statistic by offering military spouses career continuity and opportunity for advancement they miss when they are required to move and change jobs every 2-4 years.

Saving on expenses is another benefit companies can get excited about. With employees coming into the

---

[5] (Williams, et al. 2020)

office less often or not at all, organizations have the opportunity to save huge amounts of money on overhead, real estate, office space, furniture, and other items that are either no longer necessary or needed in less quantity than they would be if employees came into the office every day. These costs have been quantified by Global Workplace Analytics: "A typical U.S. employer can save $11,000 a year for each worker that works remotely 2 to 3 days a week."[6] That figure is for employees who are *only* working remotely 2 to 3 days per week!

During the pandemic, many employees were successfully teleworking full time, not just part-time. Imagine what could be done with these savings: increase salaries or other employee benefits, increase profits, improve training efforts, source additional software or other tools to help employees be more productive…the opportunities are endless!

You have probably heard anecdotally that employees who telework experience fewer interruptions and are more productive. But how much more productive are remote workers? With kids and pets and life happening when you work from home, are there really fewer interruptions? One survey found respondents experience 43 minutes a day of interruptions at home, compared to an average of 78 minutes per day in the office.[7] That's a 35-minute difference EACH DAY, which adds up to nearly three

---

[6] (Global Workplace Analytics 2021)

[7] (Global Workplace Analytics 2021)

extra hours every week. More productive? Definitely.

Remote work also slashes absenteeism. Most unscheduled absences aren't exactly due to sickness. Global Workplace Analytics found, "Nearly 70 percent of unscheduled absences are due to personal or family issues, stress, and frankly, being *sick of work*."[8]. Some employees take a day off just to avoid the office for their own mental health. Think about it: if you could avoid all the extra B.S. involved with commuting, less exposure to the annoying coworkers and office politics, wouldn't you be less likely to take a day off too?

Working remotely also improves business continuity while defending against disaster disruptions. Referred to as Continuity of Operations (COOP) in the government, remote work can be an effective contingency plan in the event a disaster makes the office an unsafe place to work. It allows employees to return to productive work more quickly than those who do not have a telework option. In companies where employees are full time remote, thus geographically separated, natural disasters, snowstorms, power outages, active shooter situations, protests, and other localized events would have less impact on productivity company-wide because it would only affect the people in a specific area, while employees across the country or globe would be able to continue working normally without interruption.

Employers can have a lot to gain by allowing workers remote options, even for part of their week. Organizations can save money, promote diversity and

---

[8] (Global Workplace Analytics 2021)

inclusion, and better their talent retention. On the other side of the equation, let's look at the fun part: the personal advantages and why the option to work remotely is such an attractive benefit.

Personal Advantages to Working Remotely

Remote work comes with a host of personal advantages, mainly surrounding saving on work-related expenses and the flexibility to design a more desirable life situation. These individual benefits apply to not only you but also each individual on your team. When you multiply these benefits by each person on your team, you could lead a much happier, healthier, and wealthier team!

First, teleworking, even part-time, allows employees to significantly reduce costs related to transportation, a workplace wardrobe, and meals out. Going into the office every day can get expensive. An employee who works from home half of the time saves between $640 and $6,400 per year due to reduced work-related costs.[9] Imagine how this money saved could create some space in your budget or even boost your retirement account.

In addition to work-related expenses, remote work offers bigger opportunities to save on major living expenses such as housing and transportation. If you have the opportunity to work remotely full time without location being a factor, you could choose to live in an area with a lower cost of living, which would compound your savings several times over. If you have kids and

---

[9] (Global Workplace Analytics 2021)

work from home, your childcare options become more flexible as well.

The option to work remotely allows a wide variety of opportunities for you to design your life intentionally without being reactive to the demands of your employer. Workers who telework just a few days a week gain options for more flexibility and work-life balance in their schedule. Without the need to spend time getting dressed up in the morning and commuting to an office, remote workers tend to find more time in their schedule for much-needed sleep, exercise, and quality time with their families. Full-time, remote workers become location-independent.

Many people are restricted in their job search to look for employment within a certain geographic area or reasonable commuting distance from their house. In a dual-income household, one spouse's job is often restricted by the location of the other spouse's job. They might be 'stuck' in a particular location because of a child in school, family nearby, friends, or the desire to stay in one location due to homeownership or land. Geographic restriction can limit a household's earning potential, and location independence offers a solution to this restriction.

Location independence is powerful. It allows you to work in a job with the income and passion opportunities you seek, instead of just being convenient for the location you want or need to live in. The job market of the entire country or even the world opens up to you when all you need to do is open your laptop to go to work. It allows you to choose where you want to live based on personal factors over professional ones. You could travel the world at your leisure, without being rushed by the amount of vacation time you can take.

Location independence allows you to live wherever you want. All you need is a solid high-speed internet connection and a space to work. Stop and think about this for a moment: If you could work from anywhere, and the location didn't matter at all, where would you live? Would you live closer to family, or maybe somewhere more suitable for your hobbies? If you're a skier, you could live in the mountains just a couple miles from the slopes. Surfing? Bring on the beaches.

By taking the commute requirement out of the picture, you also gain more time in your schedule for balance between work and life. Not only do you save time on the commute, but working remotely requires less time to get ready in the morning. With the time saved, many people find more time in their day for exercise, sleep, and time with family and friends.[10] You might gain more flexible hours and the ability to set your own schedule if you work from home. Some people need to be online during core business hours to make it easier to facilitate collaboration, but others can do their work independently of others.

Now you can see the host of advantages that come with the ability to work remotely. However, remote work is not without disadvantages. Many people struggle with the lack of social connection, fall victim to their emails and instant messaging applications, or fail to

---

[10] (Global Workplace Analytics 2021)

make productive progress on the most important deliverables for their organization. The rest of this book is dedicated to helping you, as a remote leader, overcome these tactical and emotional challenges with your team in a digital environment.

Part 2: Building Trust in the Digital Environment

Chapter 3: Why Trust is Key to Remote Leadership

"People follow leaders by choice. Without trust, at best you get compliance." *—Jesse Lyn Stoner,* author of *Full Steam Ahead*

Trust is the foundation for leadership in all environments, but it becomes even more imperative in remote work where you can't physically see your team members, and they can't see you. As stated in the opening quote, without trust, the best possible result is simply compliance.

When your team lacks trust, performance suffers. Team members are less likely to stick their necks out for you, stand up for their teammates, or go the extra mile for you. Performance suffers because they constantly feel like they need to watch their back, which creates a selfish mindset. Lacking trust, your team may be suspicious of each other and of you. This is hardly a winning attitude and distracts your team from reaching their performance potential. When trust is present, your team will be more willing to put aside any differences and focus on working together to accomplish their goal.

If trust is lacking, remote teams can really struggle. However, remote work also has the opportunity to thrive when trust exists: "Remote work gives people the autonomy they want from their roles, knowing their manager trusts that they can be productive at their own pace and on their own schedule. Create goal-based performance tracking so it's not about the hours in a day but the results."[11]

Job autonomy is also a strong protective factor against workplace burnout. Those who transitioned from in-office to remote work abruptly may experience anxiety because employees may not feel like their boss can see their performance. Taking the focus away from hours input per day and setting goal-based performance factors can help reduce this stress and performance anxiety.

As leaders, we need to extend trust to our team members in order for them to trust and perform for us. By proactively setting performance priorities with your team (which I'll cover in part three), you can extend trust to your team. Creating an environment of trust is imperative to leading a high-performance team remotely.

---

[11] (OWL Labs 2020)

Chapter 4: The Trust Equation

According to Hassan Osman, author of *Influencing Virtual Teams*, the secret formula for establishing trust is a simple function of reliability plus likability.[12]

Here is the equation written out:

$$Trust = Likability + Reliability$$

Simple, right? When I first came across this formula, I thought back to my own experience as a leader, and it made complete sense. Where I was successful in integrating both my own likability and encouraging reliability in my team members, we had plenty of trust to fuel our efforts and work together effectively. In other teams where the leader was not respected, liked, or reliable as the leader providing direction to the team, trust and performance suffered. Let's break down likability and reliability into separate components and explore ideas for you to increase each one as a leader.

Increase Your Likability

The first part of the trust equation is likability. Likability is essentially the forming of emotional ties between members of a team. You might be thinking,

---

[12] (Osman 2014)

"wait, this isn't a popularity contest, and I don't need to be liked by everyone." Yes…and no. It might not be a popularity contest but being the type of person who is generally likable is important to be able to lead people and build their trust. If you can increase your likability, you can rapidly build trust as a leader.

The fastest way to increase likability is getting to know your team members on a personal level. Ask open-ended questions and let your team members talk about themselves. By letting them talk about themselves, you're showing genuine interest in who they are as a person, which will improve their perception of you. One convenient way to increase likability is to use the few minutes at the beginning or end of meetings to have conversations about topics unrelated to work. This is a simple habit to let your team know you care about their lives.

Talk with your team face to face, if possible. Video chat is a close second to meeting in person. People can be self-conscious about using video but become comfortable with it over time. As you talk and can observe the other person's expressions and emotions, using video chat improves engagement and builds relationships. Utilizing video in your virtual conversations or meeting in person can be a great way to increase likability and understand each other's nonverbal tendencies.

Virtual teams lack the "water cooler" effect where individuals who are located in the same geographic location or work in the same building tend to have informal conversations around the water cooler, breakroom, in the hallway, or other common areas.

Without the physical proximity, chance encounters don't happen. Conversations typically aren't initiated unless either party has a work-related reason to initiate a conversation via phone call, instant message, or video chat. Encourage casual "water cooler" conversations before and after your regular team meetings. Just be sure to keep the amount of time allowed for chit-chat within reason, so other team members don't feel like you're wasting their time.

Digital leadership can have the tendency to feel way too transactional. It's easy to fall into the trap of communicating with your team only when you need something. If your only conversation is to engage in a task or transaction, it can hinder your ability to have fun with your work and be likable. Get in the habit of checking in on your team on a regular basis to see how they're doing, discuss their goals, and help them stay engaged.

In this practice, be personable, not just transactional. Share personal anecdotes about what's going on in your life. This will encourage your team to open up about their lives. The more you share, the more it promotes reciprocal sharing. This reciprocal sharing is what nurtures the forming of emotional ties between members of a team. These emotional ties are key to establishing trust in a healthy and productive work environment.

Over-communication can be another great way to increase your likability. The idea behind over-communication is the more you interact with someone, the more you tend to like and become friends with them. By over-communication, I mean reaching out to start a conversation with coworkers even if you don't have a directly work-related task to discuss. This can help prevent remote work from becoming only transactional in the work context and practices open communication. I've seen this effect in my own work relationships. Since I transitioned to a new organization in the midst of the coronavirus pandemic, meeting face to face with the members of my team was out of the question. Thus, I was forced to develop relationships digitally.

At first, it was awkward because I didn't know anyone. The rest of the team had formed their relationships in the office prior to teleworking, and I felt like an outsider. However, as I started to dig into my work tasks and reached out to different team members to ask questions, collaborate on tasks, and gather more information, I found the frequency of informal conversations increasing.

The more you communicate, the more of an opportunity there is for conversation. In my transition, I found the people who I needed to contact more often in the execution of program objectives quickly built a strong professional relationship. We became comfortable talking and working with each other through the digital environment.

Ask yourself an honest question: Are YOU a person that people genuinely like and want to work with? If you have a difficult attitude and are tough to get along with, it will be *really* hard for you to become a likable leader. This is true across all types of work environments but becomes very apparent in a remote work setting.

Similarly, if you have a tendency to avoid helping

others or frequent the refrain "that's not my job" even though you and your team have the knowledge and time to help the person with their effort, you will be avoided. Contrarily, if you are happily willing to help others when you have the time and information, go ahead and help them! If you monitor the requests for help coming into your team, agree to help where you can without adding undue burden to your team members. Others will remember your willingness to contribute and will have a more positive perception of you in the future.

Here are a few tips to become the type of person people like and want to work with:

- Take responsibility for ensuring your communications are understood

- If you say you're going to do something, follow-through and do it

- When you see someone struggling, offer to help

- When you make a mistake, take responsibility for the error *and* the resolution of said mistake

- If you see an opportunity for improvement, tactfully make suggestions

- Be thoughtful and helpful on a regular basis, regardless of your position or the position of the person you're interacting with

Most importantly, maintain a CONSISTENT and POSITIVE attitude.

Consistency in how you interact with people will establish a baseline for what they can expect from you. No one on your team will be willing to reach out to start a conversation or ask a question if they're afraid you might be grumpy or they're not sure what kind of mood you might be in. If there's a risk your reaction will be different each day, then they will most certainly avoid finding out which version of you is present when they need to chat. A consistent attitude is a predictable attitude.

Staying positive helps because if you're constantly pessimistic, there is a guarantee that interaction with you will be a drain on the other person's energy. They won't want to engage with you if you're constantly being negative or blaming others for your attitude. Positivity is much more attractive and will encourage people to reach out to you when they need something.

A positive and reliable disposition keeps your virtual office door open to communication, and it encourages your team to reach out to you often. Your team is more likely to express issues that you wouldn't otherwise hear as the manager. The more comfortable they are with your attitude, the more often they will communicate with you, which in turn, increases your likability.

Build Team Reliability

Reliability is the second critical piece to the trust equation, and it incorporates the fact that trust is a team effort. Your team relies on you, and you need to rely on your team.

It's worth mentioning here that YOU lead by example. In just about everything, your team looks to you as a standard for how they should behave.

Inside normal business hours, if you want your team responsive through commonly used communication channels such as email, instant messages, calls, or text messages, then you should also be responsive to them when they need help. Set the expectation with your team what a reasonable amount of time is to expect a response for a typical request. Obviously, this time frame will be different for urgent matters, but it's important to set the tone for what is a reasonable expectation.

Essentially, reliability is the ability and dependability of a team member to accomplish a given task. As a leader, can you be counted on to follow-through and ensure tasks are completed? Are you able to foresee what needs to be done in the future and plan your team's efforts accordingly without prompting from upper management? Can you anticipate risks and mitigate them before they become issues? These things will improve your reliability as a leader, and you can flow this level of reliability down to your team.

Always provide explicit instructions, especially for new tasks. If you fail to clearly define what you want, then prepare to get a different result than you were looking for. On the flip side, if you want to leave your team creative flexibility in how they deliver, explicitly outline the basic, non-negotiable requirements, and let them know they're free to complete the task how they see fit within said framework.

To increase reliability in your team, delegate. When you show your team you can trust them without micromanaging, it increases their level of responsibility and autonomy. Consequently, autonomy is one of the biggest protective factors against workplace burnout, and it greatly increases employee job satisfaction. Thus, if you can increase the level of responsibility of your team by counting on them, you can reduce your own stress and your team's stress. Both on remote teams and in-office teams, you can give your team members an expectation of what needs to be done by when and allow them to dictate how and when they will accomplish the work. Increasing your team's level of responsibility will help you transform into a high-functioning team, and it will prevent you from bottlenecking your team's progress.

When you do count on others, follow up with them, especially when you first start increasing their responsibility. Check in on them mid-task to see how their progress is coming. This may be needed for newer team members, and you can back off to avoid micromanaging as they gain more confidence. Are they still clear on the instructions, or do they have clarifying questions? Have they encountered any tasks they might need help with? Do they have all the connections and resources they'll require to accomplish the task? Are they still on track for the deadline, and is the deadline reasonable for the work not yet complete? Are they getting cooperation from any additional team members of whom they require assistance? Take on a supporting role to help get them everything vital for success, and then let them fly.

Trust in a remote work environment enables your team to perform at their highest potential. You can build trust as a remote leader by increasing your likability and reliability. Encourage informal conversations to build relationships within the team and an openness to help one another and outside organizations as needed. Increase the reliability of your team members by setting clear expectations and counting on them to work autonomously and complete the effort by the deadline. As you practice the loop of increasing responsibility and following up to check results, you will improve the reliability of your team and build trust.

Chapter 5: Connect Your Team with Purpose and Transparency

Purpose and transparency are two additional tactics you can integrate to build trust in your team and the people you influence. Purpose connects the reason behind the execution of your job. Transparency helps people understand the world from your point of view and gives insights into why you make the decisions you do. Transparency can be especially challenging in a remote work environment because your team won't see most of the work you do or the decisions you make unless you communicate those challenges. Both purpose and transparency are important building blocks of trust.

Connect the WHY

If your team doesn't understand why it exists or what the purpose is, then you're failing them as a leader. In his book, *Start with Why*, Simon Sinek explains, "People don't buy WHAT you do, they buy WHY you do it."[13] Without the greater reason behind your mission or purpose, the WHY of *what your team does* will be lost. As a leader, you need to make sure each and every individual can connect the WHY to what they do. They need to know how the tasks they execute on a daily basis contribute to the greater purpose of your team and your organization.

---

[13] (Sinek 2009)

With remote work, employees and tactical teams can easily feel disengaged from executive leadership and the company mission. Leadership by walking around and in-person events to connect are not a feasible option. Thus, it is imperative to find methods to re-connect all levels of the organization through events such as virtual town halls or giving executive leaders the opportunity to jump into tactical team meetings occasionally to foster connection.

Everything you do—and everything your team does—should have a reason. If you can't connect something you do back to the purpose of your team or organization, then should you really be doing it? Even if the WHY behind a task is to develop an individual or build team unity, you can further connect that WHY to the organizational mission. If individuals on the team improve or the team functions better, they are better able to contribute to the organizational mission and make things happen. If a meeting doesn't have a purpose aligned with achieving your goals and objectives, then it's an unnecessary meeting. Tasks that don't support your team's mission are superfluous tasks.

An important caveat here: the purpose of the meeting CAN be to connect and provide team members the chance to air concerns, frustrations, and questions. When working remotely, it is imperative to set aside protected time for addressing and hearing your team directly.

Most importantly: if a task DOES serve team goals and objectives but the individual assigned doesn't understand how it contributes to those goals, then the individual will see the task as unnecessary and give their effort accordingly.

This is where you bring value as a leader. Communicate the meaning behind everything you do—especially mundane or seemingly unnecessary tasks. In a remote work environment, implied meaning is easily lost. It is vital to explicitly communicate the WHY. Team leaders are not just managing people but also a specific goal or outcome. When you regularly connect the reason behind the action, your team will start to learn to do the same. When they can connect the WHY to their work, it will increase their job satisfaction, buy-in, and eagerness to do the work required of them.

Here's a cheat code for communicating the WHY behind your requests: Use the word "because" in your communication.

One word. It's really that simple. If you get in the habit of using the word "because," doors will open for you and your team. This is somewhat a hack to human behavior.

According to Robert Cialdini, "A well-known principle of human behavior says that when we ask someone to do us a favor, we will be more successful if we provide a reason. People simply like to have reasons for what they do."[14] Transparency, that's it! People just want to have a reason behind what they're doing.

Using the word "because" is especially important if you're a leader with little to no formal authority.

---

[14] (Cialdini 2006)

Despite leading teams for several years, at the time of writing, *I have not yet formally supervised anyone I've led*. I have been formally designated as the leader of a team before, but I was not responsible for writing the performance report for anyone on my team.

Remote work has increased the opportunity for informal leadership. In this environment, even more than in the office, we need informal leaders to step up and take initiative. Even without a formal designation as a supervisor or manager, you can offer to lead small efforts and increase your responsibility. This is an opportunity to provide more value to your organization and develop your skills for future promotions. Use the word "because" to help communicate your requests and influence people whom you don't formally lead.

Transparency Builds Trust

Transparency in how and why you make decisions as a leader can drive the culture on your team. Encouraging transparency can build trust and openness among your team members, and lack of transparency can destroy trust.

Being transparent with your team can help them understand why you act in a certain way and make the decisions you make. Followers might not have all the factors from your point of view. Intentional transparency is necessary in a remote environment because otherwise, your followers won't see all of the inputs to a decision, only the consequences and how it impacts them.

When you are transparent and can explain what your possible choices for a given decision are, the consequences and tradeoffs of each option, and the reason you chose the decision you made, can help your team understand the motivations behind your decision. When you do this regularly, your team will come to that you make decisions with the right intentions, and they will question your decisions less. After you build this trust, your team will have confidence in your decisions, even without knowing all the reasons behind it.

When you start being open and transparent, it starts a contagious chain reaction in your organization. Your example of transparency encourages others to also be open and honest. The more people do this, the more it shows others that it's safe to do the same.

In the midst of the 2020 coronavirus pandemic, it was extremely important to help employees feel safe from a job security stance. This is still very prevalent in employee's minds with the worry that some businesses won't recover from the pandemic and the continued risk of losing their jobs. You might feel a shift in your organizational culture when you instill transparency and trust in your team.

In my transition to a new organization mid-pandemic, my organization also got another leader a few levels above me. He was also transitioning in as the leader of a geographically separated organization consisting of around 1,800 people. In the midst of an uncertain situation, he was challenged with building trust in a digital environment. Several times in the first six months, he held virtual live sessions where he discussed what was happening in the organization, plus answered questions about our mission and the status of remote working.

One of the keys to this live session was the use of video, so his organization could see him speak and begin to learn his mannerisms, even though it wasn't a two-sided conversation. He explained what the plan was going forward and was transparent about the fact that much of the plan was dependent on how the pandemic situation would unfold, which was largely out of his control. Even though he didn't have all the answers at the time, his transparency and honestly instilled trust in his followers and communicated that he had an eye on the situation and was doing what he could for us. He built trust by giving us all the information.

Part 3: Tactics for Delivering Results in a Remote Work Environment

Chapter 6: Define Your Team's Priorities

Once you have a solid foundation of trust among your team, then you can focus on providing value to your organization through defining and prioritizing the key activities that will make a difference in your company. Creating results matters even more in a remote work environment than in an in-office environment because your boss can't see you physically working. He or she will only see the outcomes you produce.

You become valuable to your organization when you focus on the priorities that make progress or 'move the needle.' Your value does not come from how many emails you send, how many phone calls you make in a day, or how many hours you spend in meetings over the course of the week. Being "busy" doesn't necessarily mean you are creating value. Busy people like to feel like they are important, but unless they're filling their schedule with priorities, they're kidding themselves. Results and outcomes are what ultimately matter.

Understanding your role in your organization is paramount to reducing some of the anxiety connected to remote work when you lack clarity on what you are supposed to be doing. You might worry about whether you are not doing enough or doing too much and risking burnout.

In order to escape the anxiety and uncertainty around unclear expectations, you need to proactively focus on what matters for the role you are in. To do this, first, define your mission. Start with your company, organization, or team mission. Then define how your specific role connects to that mission. How does your team contribute to the mission of your company or agency? Once you know how your team contributes to your larger organization, you can determine the key activities that create results for your team. Think about why your company pays you and your team to do what you do.

Here are some probing questions to help you with this thought process and clarify your priorities:

- What does your company expect to get in return for paying you?

- Why does your company NEED you?

- Why does your team exist, and what is their ultimate purpose?

- What outcomes does your team produce?

- What activities create results for your team?

- What are your team's key performance metrics?

Your team's key performance metrics will help you hone in on what's important to your organization. This part of the process is paramount because it helps you determine what tasks should get most of your professional energy.

It is worth scheduling a meeting with your boss to go over expectations and help you define exactly what your priorities are. On what basis is your performance measured or quantified? How do you know if you are successful in your position? Have this discussion with your supervisor and consider their input. Are you on the same page? Do your priorities align? Discuss any differences of opinion and come to an agreement on the professional priorities for your position and the purpose of your team so you can guide their activities.

After you clearly define the top priorities for your position and your team's performance, then it's time to execute.

Chapter 7: Relentlessly Execute Priorities

Once you define your priorities and you're clear on which activities bring the most value to your remote work week, then it's time to relentlessly execute. By relentlessly execute, I mean constantly, repeatedly, steadily, time and time again, you will implement, perform, and enforce the tasks that are the reason you are paid the big bucks. You won't let your email or someone else drive your agenda. You will intentionally set and execute your mission and your team's mission without derailment, regardless of your work environment.

When you execute the strategies of prioritizing tasks and using time blocking to accomplish them, you will see dramatic leaps in productivity and output among your team. This efficient, results-oriented output will reduce the performance anxiety around working remotely, help your team feel secure in their jobs, and give upper-level management confidence in your ability to lead a team without being physically located in the same space as them.

By Monday morning, you should begin your week knowing what your major weekly priorities are. It is critical to start the week with a clear idea of what you'll be working on because if you don't, your inbox will quickly fill up with other people's priorities, and you'll be left on Friday wondering what happened to your week.

Set yourself a calendar reminder within the first 30 minutes to 1 hour of the first day of your week to define and plan the most important activities for the week. Another option is to establish a weekly stand-up meeting, which I'll cover in the next chapter. Your most important activity might be a big client meeting you need to bring your A-game to, or maybe it's a deadline for a document.

What deliverables are going to define your week? Is there anything you need to accomplish this week to set you up for success next week and beyond? Take these, plus your calendar into consideration and set your top priorities for the week with three categories:

1. Tasks you absolutely need to finish this week, and if everything else falls apart, at least you got this one (or two) done.

2. Tasks you really should finish this week, but you could figure it out if they had to get pushed to next week.

3. Tasks that don't need to be done this week, but it would be nice to start making progress on them, so you're not scrambling later.

Once you categorize your tasks into these three categories, you have organized your priorities for the week. Category 1 gets the most attention, especially early in the week. Don't move on to category 2 tasks until the first one is taken care of. After your category 2 tasks are well underway, then you can look ahead to the last category.

The more you practice this, the less you'll have in category 1 because you will have worked on them in earlier weeks. You'll also accomplish more as you get in the habit of focusing and executing YOUR priorities instead of unintentionally chasing someone else's priorities. After a few weeks or months of regularly establishing and knocking out these big-ticket items, you'll feel more accomplished, motivated, and excited about tackling the next tasks on your list.

Now that you are clear on your priorities for the week, it is time to eliminate distractions. What are you doing during the week that doesn't add value to your mission? Are there any meetings filling up your schedule where your presence isn't actually required? Maybe you don't need to be there at all, or maybe you're only there to stay 'in the loop.' If the latter is the case, then have the meeting organizer send you the meeting minutes afterward. It'll still keep you in the know, but it will drastically free up your schedule if you can clear out a few of the recurring weekly meetings that don't necessitate your attendance.

Sometimes we can't eliminate all of those pesky side tasks (I'm looking at you, mandatory annual training), but we can do our best to minimize their impact on our schedule by knocking them out in a focused manner rather than allowing them to drag on all day. If you find yourself getting distracted by all these 'extras' that you can't eliminate, try to accomplish them all in one block of time or one day to minimize transition time.

For example, if you have a bunch of appointments that need to be taken care of, try to schedule them all in one day or between two already scheduled obligations that have enough time between them. If you have meetings every other hour all day, it is REALLY hard to accomplish anything of value in the downtime. However, if you schedule all of your meetings back to back in the afternoon, then you have a solid chunk of time in the morning to tackle your priorities.

How to Use Time Blocking for Focus

One way you can protect and maximize your productive time and focus is through the use of time blocking. Time blocking can be a very useful tool when working from home because it can prevent you from getting distracted from the task at hand. Essentially, time blocking is setting a meeting with yourself for a block of time in your calendar, with a predetermined objective for each period of time.

The time blocking method breaks your day into chunks of productive time for your deep, high-performance work. This could be writing documents, preparing an important presentation, or working on a high-value project. Maybe you're working on setting the vision for your team or writing performance reviews. Time blocks can range from 15 minutes to a few hours.

When establishing your time blocks, design each block for the length of time, it will realistically take to accomplish the given task. If you give yourself too much time, you risk getting yourself distracted. With too little time, you won't be able to accomplish your task. Just enough, and you'll be forced to stay focused. Time blocking is basically setting artificial sprint deadlines for yourself to encourage productivity.

I have personally found I can accomplish far more when I set specific tasks for specific chunks of time, rather than writing a list of all the tasks I would like to finish by the end of the day. This helps you ensure you actually finish what you need to get done by the end of your workday, so your work doesn't bleed over into your home life. With remote work, the boundaries between work and home are blurred, and you might be easily tempted to finish up "just one more thing" before logging off at the end of your scheduled hours. Time blocking can help you finish your priorities on schedule and make a clean shift to home life at the end of the day.

In scheduling blocks of time in your day for productive work, build breaks into your schedule to help you stay on task and focused. If you try to focus on one thing for more than one hour without a scheduled interruption, your brain will actually get bored and wander. In essence, schedule in a break, or your brain will force you to take one anyway. I like to keep a large glass of water or a water bottle within arm's reach at all times when I'm working because I unconsciously sip on it.

This actually serves two purposes. The first and most obvious is that I drink more than the recommended daily water intake every day, and I stay hydrated. The second is that my bladder forces me to get up from my computer and take a break at least every 1-2 hours. When I get up for these short breaks, I can use the restroom, stretch, and refill my water bottle. It's just enough time for my brain and body to reset and refocus on the task at hand without dramatically cutting into my productive time.

During your time blocks, SHUT DOWN your email and instant messenger if you are continually interrupted. You can shut these down for 1-2 hours at a time without any major impact on your reachability, but it will dramatically improve your ability to focus and deliver results during your time blocks. If someone urgently needs to reach you in that given time, they will find a way…trust me.

Completely shut down and close out your email, don't just minimize it. The constant interruptions and email previews will swiftly take your attention away from the project you're working on. Breaking your flow can result in a significantly longer time to complete a task: "It takes an average of about 25 minutes (23 minutes and 15 seconds, to be exact) to return to the original task after an interruption."[15] Even if this just involves glancing at an email or text message for 30 seconds, it takes longer than 20 minutes for your brain to focus back on the task at hand.

Designate time blocks specifically to address issues and respond to emails AFTER you've completed your productive work each day. If your boss expects you to be instantly responsive, negotiate for a more productive time and explain why you may have a delay in response. Once your productivity and output start to soar, they'll likely have no issues with you shutting down your email for a couple of hours. You can help other people with their priorities as needed after you finish what you set for your time block. It's just like putting on your own oxygen mask first before helping a child. If you

---

[15] (Thorne 2020)

are never able to finish your work, then it would be hard to find time to help others because you're constantly worried about your own deadlines.

Execute your defined priorities by assigning the most important tasks to specific time blocks in your week. Focus and eliminate distractions during your time blocks by closing your email and messaging applications during your time block to protect your flow. Delivering results in a consistent manner will boost your confidence and job security while working remotely and instill the value of results in your team as well. Once you get in the habit of focusing and getting your high-priority projects accomplished, then you'll have time later in your day to assist other people with their priorities, respond to emails, and attend meetings.

Chapter 8: Compel Team Focus with a Weekly Stand-Up Meeting

A weekly stand-up meeting is a simple and effective way to compel your team to focus on the most important deliverables and stay productively engaged. By establishing a weekly recurring meeting, you will systematize the act of prioritizing value. Every Monday morning, each team member will be obliged to identify what their top 1-2 projects or tasks are for the week. It knocks off the weekend dust and brings the highest priorities front and center to start the week. The weekly stand-up meeting also gives a remote team the chance to connect and build engagement right at the beginning of the workweek.

This process also creates group accountability because each member states out loud what he or she will be working on during the week in front of the team. No one wants to say, "I have nothing going on; I'll just wait until my inbox fills up," or "I'm just going to see if I can survive through all these meetings on my calendar." People aren't going to say those things because they don't want the appearance of being lazy or not contributing. Yet, this is what so many people end up doing for their ENTIRE work week, week in and week out, until they have wasted their time away without accomplishing anything of value and chasing other people's priorities.

Working in a digital environment can lead to

becoming a little TOO comfortable. Creating group accountability around results can help reduce that complacency. Even though some of us might feel that way once in a while, the weekly stand-up can help us snap out of our funk and get back into work mode.

Stand-up meetings have the double benefit of keeping everyone gainfully employed in their role. If one of your team members doesn't have enough work to do (or, on the converse, too much work), a weekly stand-up can help you identify which team members are overburdened and which ones have some time on their hands to take on an additional project. Without communicating weekly workloads in a remote work environment, you as a leader might not know who is overburdened and who doesn't have enough to do. It also gives you the chance to check-in on your team mentally.

Remote work can leave us disconnected at times, so the stand-up meeting is a good time to check-in with everyone. How is everything in their life going? Are they overwhelmed or overburdened with tasks? Do they need help or additional resources with anything on their plate this week? Does someone need to cover a meeting if another can't make it?

This can help you as a leader or supervisor regularly balance out your team's workload, keep everyone gainfully employed, and be alert for signs of burnout or workplace stress. As mentioned earlier, this can be a fantastic time for informal bonding conversation to increase likability among team members.

A First-Hand Experience with Stand-Up Meetings

When I transitioned to a new organization mid-pandemic, the team I joined held a virtual Monday morning stand-up meeting every week. At first, I HATED IT! Personally, my biggest fears are appearing as incompetent or lazy. Logically, I know that I'm neither of those things, but I get *really* uncomfortable when I am put in a situation where I appear as such. In a new job or position, it is pretty much a guarantee that the new person has no clue what is going on. As a new member of the team, I was the one without a clue.

When it came to the weekly stand-up meeting, I had no idea what I needed to focus on other than in-processing my unit and trying to learn about my new program. Everyone else in the meeting discussed the important meetings and efforts they were working on, and I understood NONE of it. They were clearly on top of their game, and I was not. When the meeting finally came around to me, I was like, "Umm...I'm going to work on completing my in-processing checklist and start some of these mandatory training classes?" This made me feel SUPER incompetent, but then again: no one expects the new guy (or gal) to understand what is happening.

Even though this experience was really uncomfortable for me, it forced me to immediately look for ways to be useful and provide value to my new organization. I knocked out my in-processing, initial training, and did research to learn about my new program. I reached out to the various stakeholder contacts my predecessor had given me and quickly addressed the elephant in the room, so to speak.

It went something like this: "Hi, I'm new, and this is awkward because we have to do everything virtually. This is a little bit about me (insert professional background, hobbies, etc.). Please tell me a little bit about you, what efforts you were working with my predecessor, and what you're working on that's applicable to my position and what I need to know about." After all, if you aren't physically present to see what is happening in an organization and no one knows you are the new person to reach out to…then no one will reach out and engage you.

Being upfront and addressing the awkwardness right away will likely garner understanding and appreciation from your stakeholders. Most importantly, it invites future communication. Proactive communication lets your stakeholders know that you're the new person they can contact when they have questions or need help. Otherwise, they may have no idea who you are because they don't run into you in the office and might not see your face as the new person. The stand-up meeting encouraged me to stay engaged with the team virtually and start contributing to team efforts. This tool can do the same for your team too.

How to Conduct a Stand-Up Meeting

Now that we've discussed how a stand-up meeting can impact the execution of your team's priorities, I will discuss how to implement this practice in your remote team.

First, as the leader, prepare for the meeting. I recommend doing this the Friday before. Have an organized way to track and display your upcoming priorities, meetings for the week that need to be covered by the team, and approaching deadlines. It is also helpful to make a note of anyone who may be on vacation or off during the week. Without physically seeing the person isn't in the office, team members might otherwise be frustrated when someone doesn't respond to their emails for a week. Once you organize the priorities, it'll provide an outline for discussion and help your team keep situational awareness of everything happening.

Next and perhaps most important, keep your meeting short. It should be NO LONGER than 10-30 minutes, depending on the size of your team. Do NOT turn it into another droning hour-long meeting, or you will lose the attention, engagement, and motivation of your team at the start of the week. The goal of the stand-up is to wake everyone up from the weekend, get the team focused, then get to work on the valuable priorities!

Keep the meeting informal. In person, this would look like gathering the team quickly in your office. In a virtual environment, this is a short team call. The supervisor or team lead (probably you) will go over the big events, deadlines, taskers, or updates needed for the week. After the overview is done, ask each team member to state their top priorities, focus, events, and projects they are working on this week. This is an appropriate time to make sure they have any help or additional resources they may need to accomplish those tasks.

After you move through each member of the team, you're done. The stand-up meeting is short, sweet, and straight to the point. Send your team out to conquer the week!

Part 4: Clear and Effective Virtual Communication

Chapter 9: Hold Meetings with a Purpose

Plenty of the tips in this book you will find as good practices for leadership both in person and virtually, but they are truly critical to operating well remotely. In the office, no one wants to show up to an unnecessary meeting, but many still do. If the meeting is unnecessary, the person working remotely might dial into the call, but they are probably still doing other work during the meeting because they are disengaged from the discussion. This is destructive for two reasons: it undermines the importance of collaboration, and everyone is less effective when trying to multitask. If the goal of the meeting can be accomplished with a quick email update, then keep it to an email!

Be cautious of over-using meetings. When you schedule too many meetings during a week (or your team is required to attend a large number of meetings with outside teams or organizations), it cuts deeply into your team's creative time blocks. If there is work or a project they need to accomplish, but their schedule is fragmented by meeting after meeting, it will be really difficult to make meaningful progress on executing the team's priorities.

Another challenge to using several meetings is scheduling across time zones. A perfect 2pm meeting your you could be during someone else's lunch break! Excessive meetings can be difficult to coordinate when you are separated by several time zones. Before scheduling another meeting, stop and assess: Will we be better off having this conversation in real-time, or would it be just as easy to send an email for everyone to review as time permits?

Ideally, your team members will have the autonomy and confidence to decide which meetings require their presence. However, when they see a meeting invitation from their supervisor, team lead, or anyone else higher than them in the leadership team, it might come with the assumption that their attendance is required. Communicate clearly about which meetings are required for whom and which are optional. This will help your team protect their creative time blocks for maximum productivity.

Meetings are a delicate balance. In many cases today, meetings are overused and abused. Many meetings include more people than necessary just to keep them "in the loop," when the conversation was really just between a few people. Everyone else can be kept in the loop with a quick summary of the conversation or meeting minutes. However, I don't want to scare you away from using real-time meetings because they are an excellent tool. The value of live human connection during meetings cannot be understated. If you haven't talked in real-time with your team in a week or two, you might need to schedule a meeting simply with the purpose of connecting to each other.

Discussing a project, task, or issue in a real-time conversation can actually save a lot of time delay from discussing something via email. Virtual meetings are a fantastic way to collaborate on a task when you can't physically sit around a table together and work on something. With today's fantastic virtual tools and screen-sharing capability, it is easy for one person to share what they're working on while other people follow along, offer suggestions, and collaborate. When working on a task that requires input from multiple people, it can save a lot of time to schedule a meeting and work together on a task, rather than each person working on a document in sequence.

Make sure the meeting has a purpose or goal to accomplish. The purpose might be to get input from three people on a project or have a conversation to get everyone on the same page about a certain issue. Whatever the purpose of the meeting is, be sure everyone is aware and comes to the meeting prepared. When scheduling a meeting, put the purpose of the meeting in the description. This lets all attendees know why they are meeting, if they need to be there, and what preparation they might need to do beforehand.

There are two types of meetings I think every virtual team could benefit from. The first is a weekly stand-up meeting to get everyone focused on their priorities and motivated to execute. The second is a regular weekly (or bi-weekly) team action item meeting to review progress on assigned tasks. Both create regular human connection, which improves employee morale and engagement.

The weekly stand-up meeting was covered in depth in chapter 8, and I think this meeting is critical to creating focus on the activities that add the most value to your team and organization. This meeting opens the door for communication by creating an opportunity to let everyone know what each member is working on and ask for help as needed. It establishes the priorities for the week and allows the team leader to steer the ship in the right direction. Stand-up gives everyone on the team situational awareness of what is happening in their section. Finally, it opens the opportunity for the informal "water cooler" conversations missed when you don't work physically in the same office and allows a natural check-in on teammates.

A regular review of on-going tasks can avoid unnecessary lost time from someone "dropping the ball" or letting a lower-priority (but still important) task "fall through the cracks." Small tasks and people are more likely to fall through the cracks when you don't see or engage with them in person, a reminder to follow up on things. I recommend keeping track of all efforts and their current status through a spreadsheet or similar tracking tool. This way, you can update it and feed the updates into slides for your meeting. Your team will know when your regular meetings are and will want to complete tasks prior to the meeting, so they have an update on measurable progress to share. This keeps progress moving forward because as they report one step complete, you can assign the next step.

While meetings can be sorely overused, they are

still a very useful tool for collaboration, especially on virtual teams. Be sure to establish and communicate a purpose for every single meeting with a stated goal. Connect with each person on your team regularly to keep them engaged on the team. Utilize the weekly stand-up to focus your team and define priorities at the beginning of the week, and follow-up with a recurring team meeting to check progress on assigned tasks and on-going efforts.

Chapter 10: Assign Responsibility

When you assign responsibility for a task or project, assign a single, specific person. If you leave a request open-ended or fail to assign a single person, then everyone will end up looking for someone else to take responsibility. Especially on virtual teams, "out of sight, out of mind" can prevent anyone from taking responsibility for a project. When you can't physically see your teammates working, it is less obvious when a project isn't getting done. It is easy to say, "well, someone must be working on it," absent of visual confirmation on a remote team. Thus, it is imperative to assign a specific person and confirm receipt with that person.

If a project or task requires the support of more than one person, still assign one person primary responsibility. This point person will ultimately be responsible for progress and coordinating action on a task. You can assign supporting individuals to help the primary individual as needed. When the team knows one person is responsible, they will look to that person to initiate the necessary activity to work on the project.

Remote work makes this a must because without a primary taking the lead, everyone can simply assume someone else is taking responsibility. This also makes it easy for you to go to one person for updates on the status of the project and coordinate any additional resources as needed. Having one person responsible is a bigger deal in a remote work environment because you only want to call one person for an update—not three before you get the whole picture.

In addition to assigning responsibility to a single person, it's also imperative to set a deadline for each task. If you fail to set a deadline, the task will take as long as it possibly can. Without a clear deadline, the task will get pushed beyond tasks that do have deadlines. Even if the task is important, it may be deemed less urgent than other tasks with set deadlines. Since you aren't in the office every day to see your boss, it is easier to forget less urgent deadlines.

Parkinson's Law is known as the tendency for work to *expand to fill the time available*. Without a deadline, there is an endless amount of time available for a task, so it will take as long as it can. Another component of Parkinson's Law, most of the effort for a task is done early on when the excitement is high. Thus, the later time spent on the task can largely be avoided by proactively establishing a deadline. Remote workers may be more inclined to push tasks down when they don't have a specific deadline because they aren't seeing their coworkers as a reminder to get it done.

As a leader, follow up prior to the deadline. This can be done during the weekly meeting. After your team has started on a task, they may have additional questions for clarification or need more information. For longer projects, you may want to check in on your team at the midway point to see how much progress they've made and determine if they need more resources such as additional personnel, funding, or information to complete their task. Then, follow up closer to the deadline to see if they can still realistically complete the project by the set deadline or if the target completion date could be adjusted without significant impact to the customer. Balance supporting your team with the resources they need without micro-managing.

Be open to negotiating timelines with your team when applicable. If, as a team lead, you aren't sure how long a task should reasonably take, then ASK! When you ask your team what a reasonable timeframe is for the task in question, then it shows you are open to working with them and their schedule. It invites them to ask clarifying questions about the task that might impact how long it will take. Also, negotiating timelines will enable you to get a more realistic picture of how long something should take. When you involve your team in setting deadlines, they will also have ownership over the date set and feel responsible for sticking with the timeline.

Another situation when you want to request input on deadlines is when you lead a cross-functional or matrix team, where some of the members supporting your team or program also support other teams. Without asking, you may not have a full picture of their workload, and they may have several other tasks with priority over yours. In a remote work environment, you may not be able to see that they are supporting three or four other teams and all the associated meetings and tasks. Gather more information to determine what a reasonable completion date would be without overstressing their workload. You will gain a tremendous amount of respect from your matrix team members when you consider their entire workload and not just the tasks they are working on for you.

One example of involving the team in determining deadlines came from my experience when I was a brand new logistics manager. At the time, I had very little experience leading engineers and had no clue how long many of their tasks would take to complete. Thus, I simply asked how long the document or approval they were working on typically takes to complete. After their response, I asked if that was a reasonable expectation for the task we were currently working on.

In this way, we were able to establish a deadline reasonable for both parties and encourage teamwork in the process. The length of time it takes to accomplish a given task may increase due to remote work because of longer response times. When you plan project schedules that rely on other people or outside organizations, build the expectation of longer response times into your plan.

Chapter 11: Tactical Tips to Clarify Email Communication

Email is the primary method of communication in today's highly digital society. In a professional environment and especially on remote teams, we communicate more through email than any other method. Email is seen as a widely accepted means of formal or semi-formal communication. Just as mailing a signed letter used to be an accepted means of formal communication, now a digitally signed email carries the same effect. Email is the most common means of communication across disciplines, private industry, government, various cultures, and different countries. Thus, it deserves adequate attention, with an entire chapter devoted to tips for clarifying email communications. Clear emails are imperative in a remote work environment because you can't just walk over to someone's cubicle for clarification, and most people won't pick up the phone to ask you what you meant. They will interpret what you write at face value.

First and foremost, I have a newsflash for you: NO ONE READS YOUR EMAILS ANYMORE. Most people quickly scan their emails to get the point of the message. With boatloads of emails flooding our inboxes every day, there is a greater chance your email could be lost in the flood.

The recipient of your email will most likely just scan through your message, maybe read the first sentence, and pick out a few keywords to make a judgment as to whether your email warrants further reading. If not, their cursor finds the "Delete" button. If you want the recipient of your email to truly comprehend the message and priority you're trying to communicate (or at least increase the chances of them receiving the message you intended), then the following tips will be valuable to streamline your email communication.

Keep it Simple

Don't let the point of your message get lost in a wall of text. The best way to prevent this is to keep your message short and concise. Get to the point in your first paragraph! You can provide supporting information or additional details in subsequent paragraphs, if necessary. But if you fail to get to the point of the email in your first paragraph, you risk losing your reader.

One great way to force yourself to get to the point is to use a BLUF, or "Bottom Line Up Front." A BLUF will make it easy for your reader to see what the point of the email is before they read all the way through. If you start your email with a BLUF, it will save you time writing the email and the reader trying to decipher your message.

Highlight a call to action in your email. What do you want your reader to do once they see your email? Do you require their input, or is the email just for their information to keep them 'in the loop'? Be sure to state the call to action simply and highlight it to stand out from the rest of the email. Give the call to action a separate line in the email, *italicize,* or **bold** the call to action, or write it like this:

ACTION: Respond to questions by Thursday this week.

Without a call to action, your reader may be unsure why you sent the email, what you want them to do (if anything), and their confusion will likely result in them doing nothing.

Use the Subject Line

Subject lines exist for a reason. The subject line is intended to highlight in a few keywords what the email is actually about (a.k.a. the SUBJECT). When your email lands in the recipient's inbox, they will only see the first few words in the subject line. Keep this in mind when you decide what to write in your subject line. The first few words they see will help the reader determine whether the email warrants urgent attention or if it can wait until later.

Far too many times, I see people forward or respond to emails without changing the subject to reflect what the email is really about. Sometimes an email chain is generated by an automated email with numbers or codes in the subject, and no one can tell what the email is about until they open it up. Other times, the topic of the email changes through the course of the discussion. Don't be afraid to change or tweak the subject line to reflect the true topic of the email. Use a few keywords in your subject to summarize what the email is about.

Put a deadline in the subject line, if applicable. This is most pertinent when the email is communicating a message or request with a short suspense date. When the deadline is approaching quickly, put the date in the subject line, so it is easily noticed. If the email is forwarded to one or more parties (for example, routing a document for signature), keeping the suspense date in the subject line is a great way to keep your deadline from getting lost further down the email chain.

Another key use for the subject line is providing relevant information dictated by organizational culture. For example, when I worked in supply chain as a logistics manager, my team was responsible for over 1,700 national stock numbers (NSNs). Each national stock number referred to a different part. While not all of these stock numbers had active issues, many of these items were active, and several different NSNs all had the same nomenclature (I had *hundreds* of items called "Special Cable Assembly"). The organizational culture in supply chain—and the necessity to avoid confusing conversations about completely different items— dictated that all emails pertaining to a particular part include the NSN and part number in the subject line, in addition to the topic of conversation.

Keep Your Inbox Organized

I'm still surprised on a regular basis by the number of people who never move an email out of their inbox. When receiving more than 20 emails per day (and many receive 100+ in one day), keeping your inbox organized is critical to keeping track of your emails and avoid losing messages. While working remotely, our volume of email communication has dramatically increased because of fewer in-person discussions. This enormous volume of emails can make inbox organization even more critical than before. Avoid losing important emails by creating folders in your email server and sorting emails into applicable subjects.

Personally, I like to keep an email in my inbox until I've taken the necessary action and no longer need the reminder to read a lengthy document, follow-up on a question, or complete a task. At least once per week, I review the emails still in my inbox to see if there is anything I missed that still needs to be resolved or that I need to follow-up on. Once the email is ready to archive, I put it in a folder pertaining to the topic. That way, whenever I have a question about a specific topic, I can easily jump into the appropriate folder and look up my last communications.

Keep track of your standard work or action items somewhere other than your inbox. As you have probably experienced, inboxes can quickly get swamped, and emails can get missed. Out of sight, out of mind. To avoid losing track of important efforts, action items, or other tasks, keep a log of your standard work outside of your email. My favorite method is simply using a spreadsheet to input my tasks, last update, deadline, and actions needed. I can annotate the date of the last communication and input a reasonable date to follow-up by if I haven't seen any further communication. This is especially helpful for long-term tasks that may fall off your zone of awareness after a while. Staying organized and learning when to follow-up on your emails helps you appear more competent and avoid "dropping the ball."

Chapter 12: Leading Remotely into the Future

Leading well remotely is about taking traditional leadership tactics and adapting them to accommodate the change in an accelerating digital environment. If we can learn to become more effective remote leaders, we can develop a win-win-win situation that includes benefits to employees, benefits to the employers, and benefits to the environment. Remote leadership unlocks a whole new level of opportunities when we embrace remote work culture and adapt to different circumstances. Together, we can champion the remote work culture through learning to communicate more clearly through digital tools, building trust and transparency on remote teams, consistently executing organizational priorities, and fast-tracking our vision into the future.

Learn to improve your clear communication through digital mediums. When we understand how to communicate clearly in a digital environment and use the tools readily available to us, our teams become more comfortable operating remotely. We can discover how to develop and maintain human team connection through digital tools rather than struggling to accomplish the team mission *in spite of* digital communication challenges. Communication and enhancing human connection, even across geographical space, will help us overcome the biggest challenges to remote work.

Add value consistently by learning to define and execute your organization's priorities. Much of the resistance to telework was due to a stereotypical mind picture of individuals sitting on the couch in their pajamas with a laptop. Companies and leaders thought their employees would slack off in a remote work environment, but the response to telework during the coronavirus pandemic (forced telework for many reluctant parties) proved we are just as productive—perhaps more productive—than working in the office. As a team leader, you can help your team deliver value regularly to your organization when you consistently execute priorities.

When you execute and deliver on organizational priorities—those 'big rock' efforts that really move the needle—your boss will be less concerned about the specific hours you spend logged into your laptop. This can lessen the chronic anxiety that comes from trying to do too much work for too many hours or wondering if you are doing enough work for your given position and pay. And yes, it is easy for this anxiety to go both ways in a remote work situation because the employee and supervisor can't see each other or be seen working during their productive hours. This involves a greater degree of trust, autonomy, and expectation management. A remote work model may lead us to transition our compensation structure from the traditional hours-based work input model to a more progressive performance-based work output model. A compensation model measured by outputs rather than inputs could lead to a more productive organization and reduce the vicious cycle of workplace burnout.

Teams based on trust and transparency have the greatest ability to reach their full performance potential as a remote team. Remote leaders can build and maintain trust in their teams by increasing both reliability and likability among the group. Ways to increase reliability include verifying skills, being explicit with instructions, leading by example, and counting on others. Reliability reasons that not everyone can work remotely, as it requires a degree of autonomy and ability to work without physical supervision.

Likability can be increased by making personal connections, increasing social interactions, over-communicating, meeting face to face if possible, and keeping a consistent and positive attitude. Transparency is especially important in remote work culture because your team doesn't know what is happening in the company unless you tell them. This applies to leaders at all levels. Your team needs to be fully aware of what the context and greater challenges are, even if only for awareness. Transparency builds the values of openness and honesty on your team.

I believe remote leadership can enable fantastic opportunities that only a lucky few have been able to imagine previously. We can use the tools, ideas, and reflections in this book to champion remote teams without a digital communication barrier. Our remote teams will operate comfortably and naturally within the digital environment. The future of remote work culture will allow us to effectively execute while also offering more flexibility in work schedules and more balance between work and life priorities.

As of 2020, approximately 50% of the workforce

consists of Millennials, and Generation Z is now entering the workforce as well. Making up an increasing majority of the workforce, "Younger workers expect and demand more flexibility from their jobs than previous generations."[16] With this flexibility comes a healthy work-life balance and meaningful social connection. Remote work options can help companies attract and retain the younger generations as they become a larger influence on the workforce.

Location-independent remote work options can further help organizations recruit and retain talented human capital as we progress into the future. Companies can reduce the high expense of employee turnover by offering remote work options when an inevitable family move or transition might come up. With more and more of our work operating in the digital space, commuting into the office is less of a necessity. As society makes this shift, it will become unreasonable to expect the talent and experience required by a company to congregate in the same geographic area of the country or the world. The factors leading an individual to a certain area of study or industry are highly independent of the factors that may influence their ideal location to live in.

Further, it may be impractical to continue expecting someone to uproot their family every time they are looking to develop or advance their career. Many people value stability in their friendships and personal relationships, stability for their kids in school, and stability in their home environment. Moving your life in the interest of a job can challenge all of those desires.

[16] (Ellevate 2020)

Leading remotely may enable you to develop and advance your career AND keep all the benefits of location stability if you wish. It can also create job opportunities for those who are unable to move for personal or financial reasons, thus promoting diversity and inclusion between different geographic areas, cultures, and financial classes.

Becoming a great remote leader won't be easy, but it will be worth it. Remote leadership becomes critical in any situation where we may not be able to work in person due to a pandemic, natural disaster, or any other crazy situation. Remote work can keep your organization's mission moving forward, and they need influential remote leaders to make it happen without skipping a beat. Leading remotely can enable individuals and companies to embrace future trends to design a better world and a better life. If you can learn to provide value to your organization no matter where you are in the world, YOU will become an extremely valuable asset to your company. We always need more leaders in the world. Succeeding in the future of our increasingly digital world will require more motivated remote leaders.

Are you ready to lead your team into the future of remote work?

Thank you for Reading!

I hope you enjoyed *Leading Remote Teams: Embrace the Future of Remote Work Culture*. The ideas in this book started out as just that—ideas mulled over as the meaning of remote work evolved. Then, it quickly became a passion project. Before I knew it, the book had practically written itself as the ideas spilled from my head onto the keyboard. Several people close to me were surprised at how quickly I was able to write the book. When something needs to be said, words come easy!

This book is only the start of the conversation. As an author, I'd love to hear your feedback. All of it—praises, recommendations, and critiques! You can write me at **alexis.gerst@gmail.com** and visit my website.

Finally, I need to ask a favor. If you're so inclined, it would mean the world to me if you would post a review of *Leading Remote Teams* on Amazon or GoodReads. Loved it or hated it—I'd just like to hear what you think! Very few people actually leave reviews, so yours holds more power than you may think. If you can spare two minutes, please head to ***www.alexisgerst.com/bookreview*** and you'll be redirected to the Amazon review page. Thank you so much for reading and spending this time with me!

In gratitude,

Alexis Gerst

Connect with the Author

Visit Alexis online at ***www.alexisgerst.com*** or connect with her on LinkedIn.

Bibliography

Baker, Mary. "Gartner Survey Reveals 82% of Company Leaders Plan to Allow Employees to Work Remotely Some of the Time." (July 2020). https://www.gartner.com/en/newsroom/press-releases/2020-07-14-gartner-survey-reveals-82-percent-of-company-leaders-plan-to-allow-employees-to-work-remotely-some-of-the-time.

Cialdini, Robert. *Influence: The Psychology of Persuasion.* Harper Business, 2006.

Cohen, Rachel. "Air Force Vice Chief: Nearly One-Third of Employees May Permanently Telework." (September 2020. https://www.airforcemag.com/air-force-vice-chief-nearly-one-third-of-employees-may-permanently-telework/.

Ellevate. "Millennials Want A Healthy Work-Life Balance. Here's What Bosses Can Do." (July 2020). https://www.forbes.com/sites/ellevate/2020/07/23/millennials-want-a-healthy-work-life-balance-heres-what-bosses-can-do/.

Global Workplace Analytics. "The Business Case for Remote Work." *Global Workplace Analytics* (January 2021). https://globalworkplaceanalytics.com/wp-content/uploads/edd/2021/01/The-Business-Case-for-Remote-Work-2021-Report-Final-Web-1.pdf.

Knoll. "Flexibility for Volatility." *Global Workplace Analytics* (May 2018). https://globalworkplaceanalytics.com/wp-content/uploads/edd/2018/05/Knoll_HOK_Defense-Industry.pdf.

Mcfeely, Shane, and Ben Wigert. 2019. *This Fixable Problem Costs U.S. Businesses $1 Trillion.* (March 13). https://www.gallup.com/workplace/247391/fixable-problem-costs-businesses-trillion.aspx.

Osman, Hassan. *Influencing Virtual Teams: 17 Tactics That Get Things Done with Your Remote Employees.* CreateSpace, 2016.

OWL Labs. "State of Remote Work." *Global Workplace Analytics* (December 2020). https://globalworkplaceanalytics.com/wp-content/uploads/edd/2020/12/State-of-Remote-Work-2020-Owl-Labs-Covid.pdf.

Sinek, Simon. *Start with Why: How Great Leaders Inspire Everyone to Take Action.* Portfolio, 2009.

Thorne, Blake. "How Distractions At Work Take Up More Time Than You Think." (February 2020). http://blog.idonethis.com/distractions-at-work/.

Williams, Rosemary, Joe Mariani, Adam Routh, Akash Keyal, and Megan Hill. "Military spouse unemployment." *Deloitte Insights* (July 20). https://www2.deloitte.com/us/en/insights/ind

ustry/public-sector/military-spouse-unemployment.html.

Printed in Great Britain
by Amazon